HEAT AND TEMPERATURE

Science Experiences

FRANKLIN WATTS, INC.
NEW YORK • 1974

HEAT and TEMPERATURE

WRITTEN AND
ILLUSTRATED BY

Jeanne Bendick

Library of Congress Cataloging in Publication Data

Bendick, Jeanne.
  Heat and temperature.

  (Science experiences)
  SUMMARY: Simple experiments introduce the basic
elements of heat and temperature.
  1. Heat — Juvenile literature. 2. Temperature —
Juvenile literature. [1. Heat. 2. Temperature]
I. Title.
QC256.B46   536   73-19885
ISBN 0-531-01438-X

HEAT AND TEMPERATURE

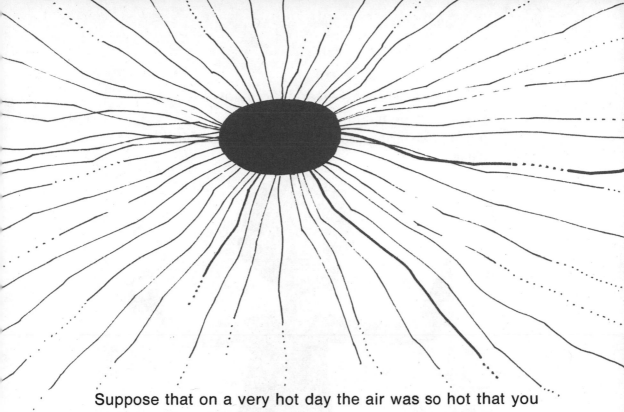

Suppose that on a very hot day the air was so hot that you decided to go to the beach.

On the way you stopped for a hot dog and it was so hot that it burned your tongue.

When you walked down the beach, the sand was so hot that it hurt your feet.

Then you ran into the water. The water was so cold that it made you feel cool all over.

WHAT DO YOU THINK?

Why did the air feel hot?

Why did the hot dog and the sand feel hot?

Why did the water feel cool?

When you say that the sand feels hot
or the water feels cool,
you are comparing them with something. What?
YOURSELF!

Hotter than what?

Colder than what?

Hotter than
your skin

Colder than
your skin

8

You compare like that all the time.

The sand feels hot because it is hotter than your skin. The water feels cold because it is colder than your skin. When you pick up a piece of hot pizza, what is it hotter than? When you eat ice cream, what is it colder than?

THINK FOR YOURSELF

After you have been in the water for a while, does the water feel as cold as it did when you first jumped in?

Why not?

Has the temperature of the water changed?

What has happened?

9

Fill a bowl with hot water. (Make it hot enough to feel hot, but not hot enough to burn you.)

Fill another bowl with very cold water. Maybe you can put some ice cubes in that bowl.

Fill a third bowl with water at room temperature. (When you need room-temperature water, fill a bowl with tap water ahead of time and let it stand for an hour. It will become the same temperature as the room.)

Now put your right hand in the hot water and your left hand in the cold water. Leave them there for a minute.

Then put both hands in the room-temperature water. How does it feel? Warm to the left hand? Cool to the right hand?

THINK FOR YOURSELF

Why does it feel that way?
Can the same bowl of water be both warm and cool?
Can it have two different temperatures?

WHAT IS TEMPERATURE?

Temperature is the measure of the hotness or the coldness of an object.

When you say that something is hot or cold, you are talking about its temperature. In everyday talk, you are saying how that thing feels to you.

You can compare two things and decide which one feels hotter. You can decide that the soup is hotter than the cocoa, or that the ice cream is colder than the apple.

When you are talking about temperature, which tells more about "how hot"—
if you say,"The soup is hot,"
or if you say, "The soup is hotter than the cocoa."?

THINK SOME MORE

Does either way tell somebody *just* how hot the soup or the cocoa is? How can you do that?

13

MEASURING TEMPERATURE

You can use a thermometer to measure exactly how hot something is.

If you took a thermometer and measured the temperature of a cup of sand from the beach and a cup of water from the ocean, the thermometer could measure how hot the sand was and how hot the water was. You could read "how hot" on the scale of the thermometer.

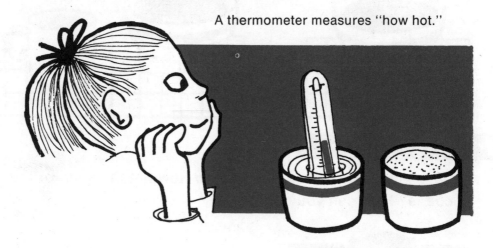

A thermometer measures "how hot."

If you took a thermometer and measured the temperature of a cup of soup and a cup of cocoa, you could read, on the scale of the thermometer, which was hotter and how much hotter it was.

Hotness is measured in degrees. This is the symbol for a degree °.

14

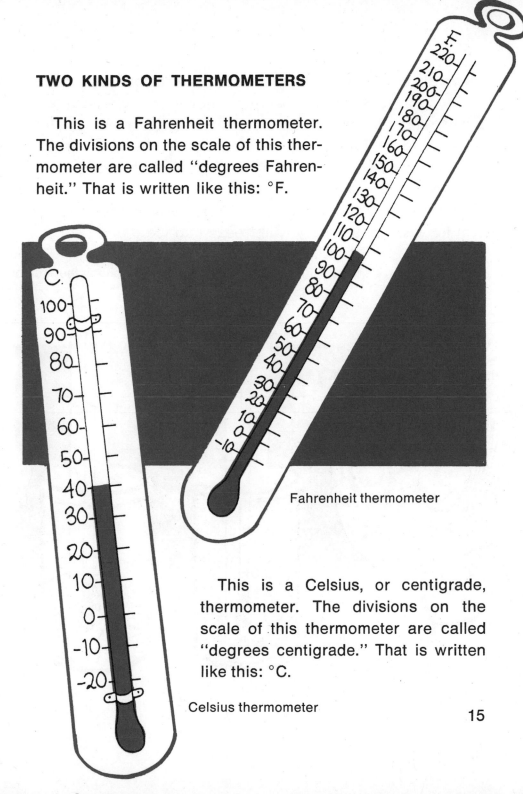

TWO KINDS OF THERMOMETERS

This is a Fahrenheit thermometer. The divisions on the scale of this thermometer are called "degrees Fahrenheit." That is written like this: °F.

Fahrenheit thermometer

This is a Celsius, or centigrade, thermometer. The divisions on the scale of this thermometer are called "degrees centigrade." That is written like this: °C.

Celsius thermometer

15

Both thermometers measure temperature, but they have different scales. If you put each thermometer into a separate jar with a little water and lots of ice cubes, after a few minutes the liquid in the Fahrenheit thermometer will be at the freezing point of water, 32° on its scale. The liquid in the Celsius thermometer will be at 0°, the freezing point of water on *its* scale. When the temperature of water stays at the freezing point for a while, the water will freeze into ice.

Celsius thermometer   Fahrenheit thermometer

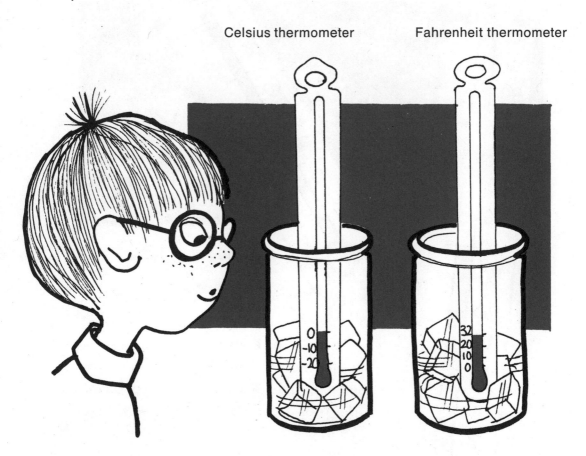

Does the scale of measurement change the temperature of the water? Is the water temperature different in the two jars? Change each thermometer into the other jar and see for yourself.

On the Celsius thermometer scale the freezing point of water is 0° and the boiling point of water is 100°. There are 100 degrees between the freezing point of water and the boiling point.

On the Fahrenheit thermometer scale the freezing point of water is 32° and the boiling point is 212°. There are 180° between the freezing point and the boiling point.

You can do much more with this book if you have a Celsius laboratory thermometer, or a double-scale laboratory thermometer. They don't cost much at a hobby shop. Household thermometers aren't safe at high temperatures. Cooking thermometers have no low temperature scale.

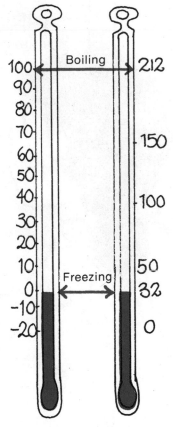

Celsius
thermometer

Fahrenheit
thermometer

Which thermometer do you think is easier to use?

When you are using a Fahrenheit thermometer, to change degrees F. to degrees C., subtract 32 and divide by 1.8.

To change degrees C. to degrees F., multiply by 1.8 and add 32.

18

Look at a weather thermometer, a medical thermometer, a cooking thermometer, and any other thermometers you can find. Can you tell which scale each one uses? Which scale do you think scientists use?

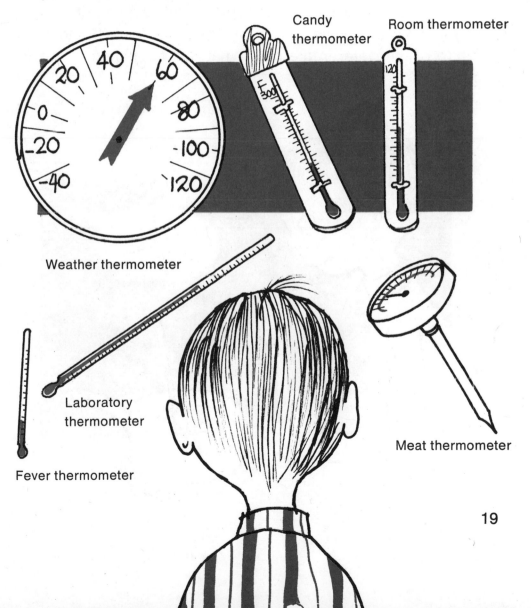

Candy thermometer

Room thermometer

Weather thermometer

Laboratory thermometer

Fever thermometer

Meat thermometer

19

Take two pans and put a cup of room-temperature water in each one. On the Celsius thermometer the temperature would be about 25°. (How many degrees on the Fahrenheit thermometer?)

Put one pan on the stove and put the heat on under it. Stir the water. In two minutes, turn off the heat. Measure the temperature of the water in the pan. What has happened to the temperature?

Start with water at room temperature.
Add heat.

20

Put some ice cubes in the other pan. Stir the water and ice cubes. In two minutes, measure the temperature of the water in the pan with the ice cubes. What has happened to the temperature?

Start with water at room temperature.
Add ice. What does that take away?

THINK FOR YOURSELF

What happened to the water in the pan on the stove?
What happened to the water with the ice cubes in it?
How do you make things hotter?
How do you make things cooler?

MAKING THINGS HOTTER

You make things hotter by adding heat.

You can add heat from a gas stove to a pan.

You can heat a can with a candle, or you can heat a room with burning wood.

You can heat a whole house with burning coal or oil.

You can add heat to a room or a pot or a house or a slice of bread with electricity.

Heat from the sun makes the earth hotter.
You can make things hotter by rubbing them together.
Any time you add heat, you make something hotter.

THINK FOR YOURSELF

What is the connection between heat and temperature?

WHAT IS HEAT?

Adding heat makes things hotter.

Heat is a kind of energy.

If someone says that you have a lot of energy, that means that you can work and play and think and grow and do a lot of other things. You get your energy from food.

Food has energy. It heats you up.

24

Fuel has energy. It can heat things up.

Wood is fuel. Coal, gas, and oil are fuels, too.

There is energy in motion. Motion can heat things up.

There is energy in the sun. The sun can heat things up.

There is energy stored in everything, even things that feel cold, like the ocean or an ice cube.

WHY DO THINGS GET HOTTER?

Things get hotter when heat comes into them.
We say that heat *flows*.

Fill a bowl with hot water. (If you measure with a Celsius thermometer, the water should be about 50°. On a Fahrenheit thermometer it would be about 122°.)
Put one hand in the hot water.
Does your hand get hot?
Are you surprised?
Probably not. It is what you expected to happen.
But why?

ONE WAY

HOTTER COOLER

Heat moves down a one-way street.

You've probably never thought about it, but it has been your experience that heat moves from a hotter thing into a cooler one, and heats the cooler thing up. Which was hotter to begin with, the water or your hand?

NOW TRY THIS

Measure the temperature of the water.
Is it still 50° C.?

THINK FOR YOURSELF

Why did the water get cooler?
Where did the heat from the water go?

WHY DO THINGS GET COOLER?

Now fill another bowl with very cold water. Measure the temperature of the water with your thermometer. See if you can make it about 10° or 15° C. If you use ice cubes, take them out when the water is cold enough.

Put your warm hand in the bowl and leave it there for a couple of minutes.

Does your hand get cold?

Are you surprised? Probably not. It is what you expected to happen. But why?

WHAT DO YOU THINK?

Did the cold from the cold water move into your hand and make it cold?

NOW DO THIS

Measure the temperature of the water in the bowl.

What has happened to it?

THINK FOR YOURSELF

How did the water get warmer?

Where did the heat to warm it up come from?

Do you know now why your hand got cold?

29

HEAT FLOWS IN AND OUT

When temperature changes, heat has flowed in or out.

If something gets hotter, heat has flowed into it.

If something gets cooler, heat has flowed out of it.

Heat always moves from a warmer place or thing to a cooler place or thing around it.

Whenever something gets warmer, heat has come into it from somewhere. Nothing just gets warm by itself.

You can use arrows to show how heat flows.

When something gets warmer, heat has moved in.

When something gets cooler, heat has moved out.

Whenever something gets colder, heat has gone out of it into something else. Heat never just disappears.

Put a cup of very hot water in the refrigerator. What happens? Where does the heat go? See if you can find out what gets warmer.

Put a piece of bread in the toaster. What happens? Where is the heat coming from? Where is it going?

Put an ice cube on the kitchen table. What happens? Where does the heat come from? What happens to the air around the ice cube?

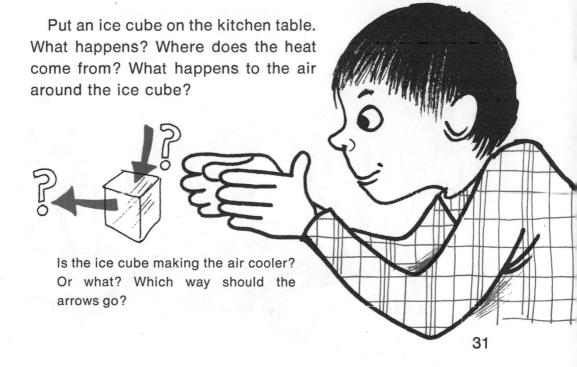

Is the ice cube making the air cooler? Or what? Which way should the arrows go?

31

HEAT FLOWS FAST AND SLOW

When something is much hotter than the things around it, heat flows fast, out of the hot thing into the cooler things.

If the temperatures of all the things are almost the same, heat moves more slowly.

Take two glasses of hot water.
Put one glass in a pan of room-temperature water.
Put the other glass in a pan of ice water.
Put a thermometer into each glass.
Measure the temperature change in each glass.
Which changes the most? How fast did it change?

32

Now leave all the water for a couple of hours. Leave the thermometers in.

When you look at the thermometers later, is the temperature in both glasses the same? What about the temperature of the water in the pans? What about the air temperature in the room?

Heat moves out of a warmer thing into a cooler one until the temperatures are the same. Heat evens out.

THINK FOR YOURSELF

Is that why very cold water doesn't feel as cold after you have been in it for a while?

Has some heat moved out of your skin?

Will the water feel the same to him as it does to you if you have been in for a while?

CAN YOU MEASURE HEAT?

Temperature is the measure of the hotness or the coldness of an object. You can measure that with a thermometer.

Measuring heat isn't as easy. But people have made up units for measuring heat, just as they made up units for measuring temperature.

The unit for measuring *temperature* in the metric system is a degree centigrade. The unit for measuring *heat* in the metric system is called a calorie.

34

A calorie is the amount of heat needed to raise the temperature of 1 gram of water 1 degree centigrade.

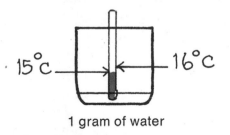

1 gram of water

When the temperature goes up 1 degree C., 1 calorie has been added to 1 gram of water.

A *calorie* is a measurement of heat. When it is spelled *Calorie* (with a capital C) it means 1000 calories. That measurement is used to measure the amount of heat in food. It is sometimes called a large calorie.

Where people do not use the metric system, the unit for measuring temperature is a degree Fahrenheit. And the unit for measuring heat is a BTU (British Thermal — or heat — Unit). A BTU is the amount of heat needed to raise the temperature of 1 pound of water 1 degree Fahrenheit.

Before you can measure how much heat has been added, you have to measure the change in the temperature of the water. How much hotter did it get? And you have to measure the amount, or *volume,* of water that has been heated.

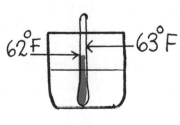

1 pound of water

When the temperature goes up 1 degree F., 1 BTU has been added to 1 pound of water.

Why should the *amount* of water make a difference when you're adding heat? If you add the same amount of heat to one cup of water or two cups of water, won't they get equally hot?

On a sunny day, take two cans, the same size and shape. (Soup cans are fine.)

36

Put half a cup of cold water in one can.

Put one cup of cold water in the other.

Stand both cans on a windowsill in the sun.

In 15 minutes, measure the temperature of the half cup of water. Measure the temperature of the cup of water. What have you found out?

How long would it take for the cup of water to get as warm as the half cup got in 15 minutes? Leave the thermometer in the cup of water to see.

THINK FOR YOURSELF

Could you invent a name for a unit of heat that raises the temperature of a half cup of water 1 degree? Could you use the same unit to measure the amount of heat that has been added to the other can?

37

HOW HEAT MOVES

How does heat move from one place to another?

Heat moves in different ways. Sometimes it moves *through* things.

TRY THIS YOURSELF

Put the bowl end of a metal spoon into a pan of very hot water. Hold the handle. In a minute or two, what do you feel? Is the handle getting hot? How?

Heat has moved from the water into the spoon. It moves through the spoon until the whole spoon is hot.

WHAT DO YOU THINK?

If you keep holding the spoon, will the heat keep moving, into your hand?

When heat moves through solid things this way, we say heat moves by *conduction.*

CAN YOU REMEMBER?

When somebody fries eggs, does the whole pan get hot, or only part of the pan? Even if it's a very big pan, could you fry an egg in any part of it? Why?

Heat flows by conduction from one part of a hot object to another.
Heat flows by conduction between two objects that are touching.

Put some very hot water in a metal mug.

Put some more very hot water in a china mug.

Put one hand around each mug.

What do you feel?

Does the heat make you want to take your hand away from one mug pretty soon? Which one?

We said that heat moves through solid things by conduction. Then why isn't the heat moving through the china mug as well as it moves through the metal one?

Heat moves better through some things than through others. The things that pass heat along well are called good conductors. Good conductors heat up and cool off fast. Metals are good conductors.

40

Some things do not conduct heat well. Objects like this are called poor conductors. Glass, wood, and air are some of the poor conductors.

TRY THIS YOURSELF

Some of these things are good conductors.
Some are poor conductors.
Can you find out which is which? Or do you know?

Another name for a poor conductor is an *insulator.* An insulator keeps heat from moving.

It is handy to know which kinds of things conduct heat well and which kinds do not, because sometimes we want heat to move easily from one thing to another, and sometimes we want to keep it from moving as much as possible.

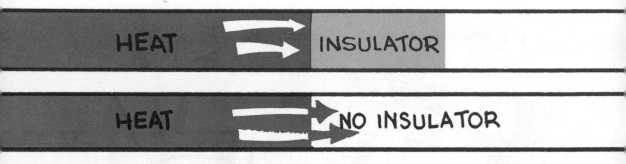

HEAT ➡ ➡ INSULATOR

HEAT ➡ NO INSULATOR

THINK FOR YOURSELF

Why are stoves and irons and pots and pans made of metal? Why do they usually not have metal handles?

You wear woolen clothes in the winter because wool is full of little air spaces, and air is a poor conductor. Styrofoam — the material that picnic ice chests are made of — is full of air spaces, too.

THINK SOME MORE

Do you wear woolen clothes when it's cold to keep the cold out? Or to keep your body's heat in?

Where would you put the arrow?
Where would it stop?

Does a styrofoam ice chest keep the cold in? Or keep the heat out?

Where would you put the arrow?
Where would it stop?

43

Walk around in the house.
Feel a glass.
Feel a rubber ball.
Feel a wooden chair.
Feel a faucet.
Feel a clay flowerpot.
Feel a skate key.
Feel a sweater.

All the things on these pages are the same temperature as the room. Your body is warmer than room temperature.

44

Take off your shoes and socks and stand on the rug. Stand barefoot on the wooden floor. Go into the bathroom and stand with one foot on the mat and one foot on the tile floor.

Which things are the good conductors? The good conductors feel cooler than the poor conductors when you touch them. Why is that? Has it anything to do with heat moving?

HEAT MOVES *WITH* SOME THINGS

Heat moves in another way when it moves in liquids, like water, and gases, like air.

Instead of moving *through* liquids and gases, heat moves them and moves with them.

Heat makes water move and it moves along with water.

TRY THIS

Put some tiny bits of heavy paper in a pot of water and put heat under the pot. Use a glass pot if you have one. It's easier to watch.

What happens to the paper as the water nearest to the heat gets hot?

Which way does the heated water move?

What happens to the cooler water at the top of the pot? Which way does it move?

46

Heat makes air move, and it moves along with air.

Put your hand over a hot radiator. Can you feel the air moving, carrying the heat?
Which way does the heated air go?
Where is the air in the room warmer?
Where is it cooler?
See if you can find out.

47

If you are heating water on the stove, the water at the bottom of the pot gets hot and rises toward the top. When the hot water comes up, it pushes the cold water at the top out of the way.

The cold water sinks to the bottom. What happens when it gets heated?

Hot and cold water keep changing places until all the water in the pot is hot.

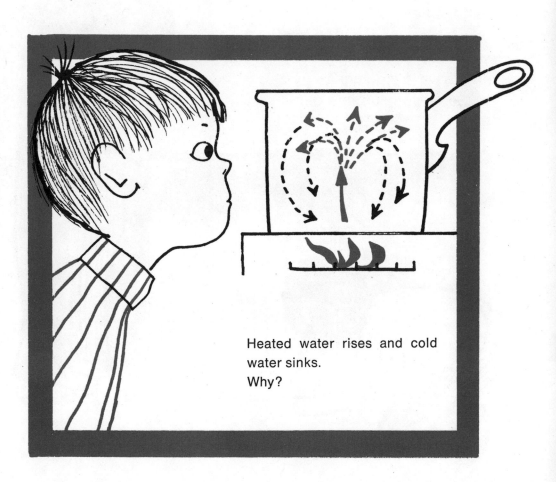

Heated water rises and cold water sinks.
Why?

The same thing happens to air in a room. Hot air keeps rising and cool air sinks. Hot and cool air change places until all the air in the room is the same temperature.

When heat moves this way, it moves by *convection*.

Hot air rises.
Cold air sinks.
Why?

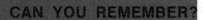

CAN YOU REMEMBER?

On a hot summer day, do thunderhead clouds grow taller and taller in the sky? What do you think pushes them up?

Put an empty balloon over the neck of a bottle, like this.

Stand the bottle in a pan of very hot water.

What happens to the balloon? Is it getting bigger? What is making it bigger?

Heat makes gases expand. They take up more room. Scientists say they increase in volume. Heat expanded the air in the bottle, up into the balloon.

50

Now take the balloon and blow it up all the way. Tie the neck and put the balloon in the refrigerator for half an hour. What happens to it?

THINK FOR YOURSELF

Why is the balloon smaller? Did the air get out? Or did something happen when the heat went out? What?

CAN YOU FIND OUT?

Do solid and liquid things expand when they are heated, and contract (or get smaller) when they are cold, too?

Why do you put a stuck jar top under hot water?

51

Read the temperature on the scale of a thermometer, then put it in a cup of hot water.

What happens to the liquid in the thermometer?

What did the heat do to the liquid?

Now put the thermometer in a cup of cold water. What happens to the liquid in the thermometer when heat goes out of it?

Try the same thing with a dial thermometer. Instead of having liquid in it, a dial thermometer has a curved strip made of two metals. (A meat thermometer is like that.)

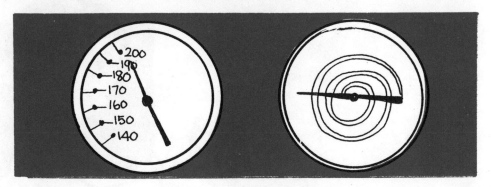

What happens to the metal strip when it gets hotter?

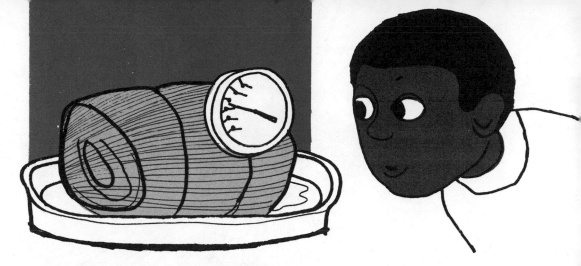

When metal gets hot, does it expand?

Read the scale to see if the temperature goes up.

What happens to the metal when the heat goes out of it?
What happens on the scale?

WHAT DO YOU THINK?

If solids, liquids, and gases did not change volume when
they were heated or cooled, could you measure temperature?

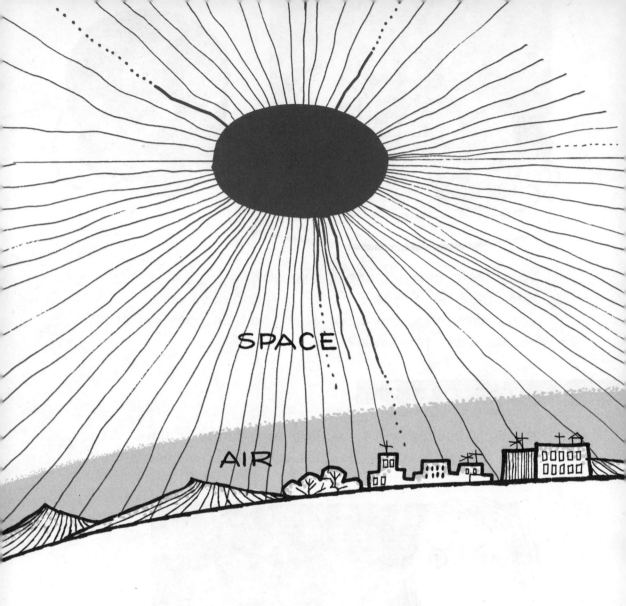

SPACE

AIR

Heat moves *through* some things and *with* other things. But most of the heat on earth comes from the sun. How does the heat get to us across millions of miles of empty space? There is nothing to move through. And nothing to move with.

54

Heat can move in another way — by *radiation.* That is how we get heat from the sun. Radiation can go through empty space. It is more like light than it is like the heat that moves by conduction or convection.

The heat-light from the sun passes through space and air without heating them at all.

But when the heat-light gets to earth it heats land and water, buildings, cars, and all the other things it shines on. And the heat from those things heats the air around earth.

WHAT DO YOU THINK?

Do other things besides the sun radiate heat?

Hold your hand *under* a radiator. (Convection makes the heat go up.) What do you feel?

Do you feel heat from a lamp when you're under it?

Do you radiate heat? How could you find out?

The sun's rays pass right through space and air and things like glass.

Sunlight is *reflected* by other things. It is bounced off, back into the air. Light-colored or shiny things like sidewalks and buildings, white hats, and tin roofs reflect the sun's heat-light. Clouds reflect it, too.

But things like tar roofs and dark clothes and plowed fields absorb the sun's radiation. They take it in. So does water.

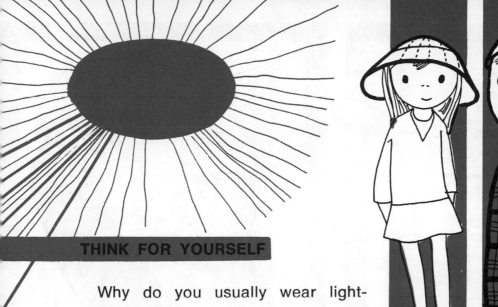

THINK FOR YOURSELF

Why do you usually wear light-colored clothes in the summer and darker ones in the winter?

Which takes in the most heat, a field covered with snow or a field covered with grass?

THINK SOME MORE

Why is a clear day warmer than a cloudy one?

Why is a cloudy night warmer than a clear one?

57

Look at these pictures. See if you can figure out where in the pictures the heat is moving by conduction, by convection, or by radiation — or maybe in more than one way.

What do you think would happen if heat did not move from one thing to another?

Could you boil water?

Could you heat a house?

Could the sun heat the earth?

HEAT MAKES THINGS CHANGE

When heat comes in or goes out, sometimes solids, liquids, and gases change from one to another.

Ice is a solid. When enough heat comes in, it changes into water.

Water is a liquid. When enough heat comes in, it changes into steam.

Where is the heat coming from?

Steam is a gas. When enough heat goes out, it changes into water.

If enough heat goes out of water, what does it change into?

Where is it going?

61

When solids, liquids, and gases take in enough heat or give off enough heat they change their form. Some solids, liquids, and gases don't have to get much hotter or colder to change their form. A lot of heat has to come in or go out to make other things change.

Which of these things change form easily?
Which change form only when a lot of heat comes in or goes out?

62

Hang a wet cloth in the air. What happens to the water? What did it change into?

Take some ice cream out of the freezer and put it in the refrigerator. What happens to it?

Put a bar of chocolate in the sun. What happens to it?

Does it take a lot of heat coming in or going out to change those things?

When things change form, do they change shape?
Do they change size?

64

A change of temperature — a big change or a little one — makes some things change form. But the thing itself doesn't really change. When things change in this way, they can always be changed back.

THINK SOME MORE

How could you change melted chocolate to solid chocolate again?

How could you change ice into water?

How could you change water into ice?

How could you change water into steam, or water vapor?

What would you have to add or take away?

65

Sometimes heat changes things and they can't be changed back.

If you burn a log, it changes into smoke and ashes. Can you change those things back to a log again?

If you bake a cake, can you change it back to batter?

If you boil an egg, can you unboil it?

If you burn gasoline to run a car, can you get the gasoline back?

Changes like these are chemical changes. They can't be changed back.

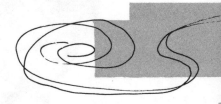

Is it a change of form or a chemical change
if you
fry an egg,
melt butter,
burn a candle,
burn a hole in the tablecloth,
freeze ice cream?

67

WHERE DOES HEAT GO?

Once heat goes out of something, you can't get it back.
Can you get back the heat that has gone from a freezing pond into the air? Or the heat from a light bulb? Or the heat from a fire?

Once something has cooled, you have to add new heat to make it hot again. Will cold soup get hot by itself? How about a cold oven?

Where does all the heat that flows out of things go?

Somewhere. Into cooler things. And still cooler things. And finally, out into space.

WHAT DO YOU THINK?

Do you think that sometime everything in the world might be the same temperature?

69

HINTS TO HELP YOU WITH SOME ANSWERS

Page 23. Things get hotter (temperature) when heat is added. Would there be temperature without heat?

Page 31. Which way does heat always flow? Could cold from the ice cube be moving into the air?

Page 37. People name all units of measurement. You could call your units *whews* or *sizzles* or anything else. Whews could measure heat as well as calories or BTUs as long as you follow the rules.

Page 43. Which is hotter, the boy or the air? Which is hotter, the air or the inside of the chest?

Page 45. When you touch a good conductor, heat moves *fast* out of that part of you into the good conductor. How do your fingers feel when they lose heat? What about your feet?

Page 51. If gas expands in a balloon or anything else when heat comes in, what happens when heat goes out?

Page 53. About measuring temperature, see what you can find out about the Kelvin scale. You couldn't measure with a Fahrenheit or a Celsius thermometer if liquids did not change volume.

Page 55. Do you radiate heat? Sometime hold your hand a few inches away from a frosted window.

Page 57. About clear and cloudy days and nights: Where does heat come from in the daytime? What could get in the way? Which is warmer at night, the earth or space?

Page 67. What can't you change back?

Page 68. Sooner or later, does heat even out? Even if it takes millions or billions of years?

Index

ABOUT THE AUTHOR

Jeanne Bendick is well known as an illustrator and the author of many science books for young people. She is a graduate of Parsons (The New School) and has taken (and given) continuing courses in elementary education.

Besides her work in books, she and her husband, Robert Bendick, design learning systems using written and graphic materials, filmstrips, films, tapes, and records.

She sometimes works on two or three projects at a time. "I find I get a fresher approach if I shift gears," she says.

As hobbies, Ms Bendick lists working, cooking, snowshoeing and looking at "little things" everywhere.